MARGRET & H.A. REY'S
Curious George
Goes to the Beach

Illustrated in the style of H. A. Rey by Vipah Interactive

HOUGHTON MIFFLIN HARCOURT
Boston New York

Based on the character of Curious George®, created by Margret and H. A. Rey.
Illustrated by Vipah Interactive, Wellesley, Massachusetts: C. Becker, D. Fakkel,
M. Jensen, C. Yu.

www.hmhbooks.com

The text of this book is set in 17-point Adobe Garamond.
The illustrations are watercolor and charcoal pencil, reproduced in full color.

Library of Congress Cataloging-in-Publication Data

Curious George goes to the beach / illustrated in the style of H. A. Rey by Vipah Interactive.
p.   cm.
Based on the original character by Margret & H. A. Rey.
Summary: Curious George has fun feeding the sea gulls at the beach and then saves the day
when he rescues a picnic basket and helps his friend overcome her fear of the water.
RNF ISBN 0-395-97834-3 PAP ISBN 978-0-544-25001-7 PABRD ISBN 0-395-97846-7
[1. Monkeys Fiction. 2. Beaches Fiction.] I. Rey, Margret. II. Rey, H. A. (Hans Augusto),
1898–1977. III. Vipah Interactive. IV. Title: Margret and H. A. Rey's Curious George
goes to the beach. V. Title: Curious George goes to the beach.
PZ7.C921642   1999
[E]—dc21
                                                    99-31534
                                                    CIP

Manufactured in China
SCP 10 9 8 7 6 5 4 3 2 1
4500448623

This is George.

He lived with his friend, the man with the yellow hat.

He was a good little monkey and always very curious. Today the man had a surprise for George. He took George to the beach.

They found a spot on the warm sand, then — another surprise!
George saw his friend Betsy. "Look, Betsy," her grandmother said,
"It's Curious George!" But Betsy did not even smile. She had never
been in the ocean before. She was scared.

"I know you're a good swimmer," the man told her. "You'll be fine once you get in the water." Feeling better, Betsy walked toward the shore with her grandmother.

George helped spread the beach blanket and set aside their lunch. He was looking forward to a picnic, but it was not yet time to eat. . . .

It was time to play! In no
time George was having fun.
He learned a new game,

he dug in the sand,

and he made a new friend (monkeys
are good at making friends).

When he took a break, George watched
the lifeguard. The lifeguard sat in a special
chair. Sometimes he blew a whistle.

And sometimes he looked through binoculars.

It looked like fun to be a lifeguard. George was curious. Could he be a lifeguard?

Before long, the lifeguard took a break. Here was George's chance!

Watching the crowd from up in the special chair, George felt just like a lifeguard. He looked through the binoculars.

There was a lot to see at the beach.

He saw sea gulls flying high above, and he saw Betsy on the shore below. She still had not been in the water. Then the lifeguard saw George. "Hey," he yelled. "That's no place for a monkey!"

George thought it was a fine place for a monkey, but he did not want to cause trouble. So he climbed down.

Back at the beach blanket, George was hungry for a snack.

No one would miss just one
cracker, thought George.

He took one out and put it
on a napkin. It looked good!

Now, if only he had
some cheese....

Uh-oh. What happened
to his cracker?

Well, he would just
have to get a new one.

George found another cracker,
then turned back around.

But now his *cheese* was gone!
Who could be taking his snacks?

George was curious. He put
down his cracker and waited.

Now George saw who was taking his treats. It was a sea gull — and he was still hungry!

George took out another cracker, and the bird took it right out of his hand!
What fun to feed a sea gull!

George saw more sea gulls down by the water. Betsy was there, too. George was curious — could those sea gulls be hungry?

Indeed, they WERE hungry! Soon a whole flock had gathered. George could not feed them fast enough. Luckily, Betsy was glad to help. Out of the basket came more crackers, cookies, a cake — and even the bread for sandwiches.

Still the birds were hungry. But when George reached for more snacks, the basket was gone! He and Betsy were having so much fun, they didn't notice the tide coming in. . . .

They didn't notice the picnic basket was floating out to sea. George felt bad — he hadn't meant to lose the basket. Could there be a way to catch it? George thought and thought.

Then he remembered the lifeguard.
George was no lifeguard, but to save the
basket he knew just what to do!

Quickly he found a float
and carried it to the water.
Jumping aboard, George
began to paddle.

He paddled out a little farther, and a little farther, and a little farther. Until, finally, he reached the basket. Betsy cheered. Then, as George paddled back to the beach, Betsy swam out to meet him!

Everyone was glad to see George safe on the shore. The lifeguard, who had seen everything from his chair, said, "That was some rescue!" George felt proud.

The man with the yellow hat picked up the basket. He was curious. "George, is this *our* basket?" he asked.

Poor George. After all that, the basket was empty! There would be no picnic on the beach, and it was all his fault.

Then Betsy's grandmother said, "Won't you join us for lunch? We have plenty—and look! Now we have a reason to celebrate, thanks to George." They did have a reason to celebrate. Betsy was

in the water — and she wasn't scared anymore. She was having fun!

After everyone joined Betsy and George for a swim, it was time to eat at last.

There were sandwiches and chips, bananas, cookies, and watermelon. There *was* plenty for everyone...and there was even a little for guests.

The end.